COMPOSER
SHOWCASE
HAL LEONARD
STUDENT PIANO LIBRARY

Jazz Delights

ORIGINAL PIANO SOLOS IN VARIOUS JAZZ STYLES

BY BILL BOYD

CONTENTS

ISBN 978-0-7935-2621-5

HAL•LEONARD®
CORPORATION

7777 W. BLUEMOUND RD. P.O. BOX 13819 MILWAUKEE, WI 53213

Visit Hal Leonard Online at
www.halleonard.com

FOREWORD

The compositions in this book were written to acquaint the student with various jazz idioms and pianistic devices characteristic of each style.

For example, A CHORDING TO CHARLIE employs a chord progression typical of the Be-Bop era.

BLUE WALTZ and THREE FOR JAZZ are examples of the slow jazz waltz and WALTZ FOR AMY contains rhythm patterns found in the fast jazz waltz.

SATIN LATIN, LATIN LOGIC and IN A LATIN ROCK MOOD have chord progressions and melodic material which illustrate the Latin Rock style.

The melodic line of ROCK SHOCK is based entirely on the notes of the minor blues scale. Jazz musicians play this scale when improvising on rock compositions.

The opening measures of BALLAD FOR AMY have a left hand bass rhythm which is typical of slow rock music.

Many cliche melodic voicings appear in NOTHIN' COULD BE FINER THAN MINOR.

HANG OUT uses chord progressions and rhythms found in the "down home" rock style.

INTRODUCTION

The compositions in this book are written in several jazz styles . . . rock, latin rock, swing, blues and the slow and fast jazz waltz. Each style requires a certain type of eighth note interpretation. Generally, slow ballads and rock pieces are played with even eighth notes as in classical music. Uneven eighth notes are played in swing and modern jazz compositions. A more precise explanation of eighth note performance appears in the box below.

The grace notes in this book are to be played on the beat together with the principal note and then stopped immediately allowing the principal note to sound alone.

PERFORMANCE NOTES

When a practice rhythm appears at the top of a composition, play the rhythm on one note while counting out loud; then, find the measure or measures that contain the rhythm and play the actual notes.

SWING EIGHTH NOTES

Eighth notes in swing style jazz are written evenly as in classical music but are played **unevenly.** Practice the following exercises to learn the proper performance of swing eighth notes.

Play and count eighth note triplets.

Tie the first two notes of the triplet together. The resulting rhythm is the swing eighth note feeling.

The triplet rhythm with the first two notes tied together may also be notated in the following manner.

Once the swing eight note "feeling" is achieved, the counting may revert back to "one and two and etc."

On your music, you'll see the following indication:

ROCK EIGHTH NOTES

In the rock or slow ballad styles, the notes are played evenly as in classical music.

On your music, you'll see the following indication:

BLUE WALTZ

Practice rhythms

SATIN LATIN

Latin Rock (play evenly)

8

Practice rhythm

THREE FOR JAZZ

Practice rhythms

1 & 2 & 3 & 4 & 1 & 2 & 3 & 4 & 1 & 2 & 3 & 4 &

A CHORDING TO CHARLIE

Moderate Swing Tempo (♫ played as ♪³♪)

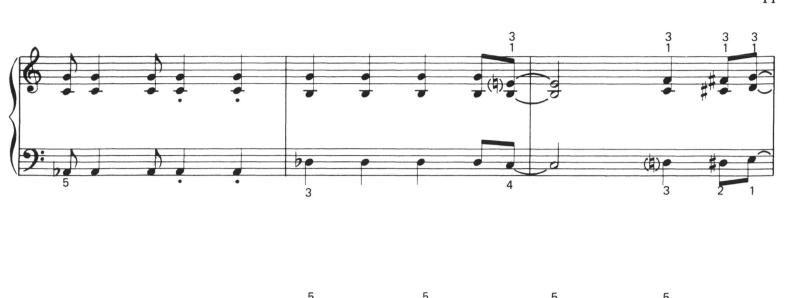

BALLAD FOR AMY

ROCK SHOCK

gradually softer

p

Practice Rhythms

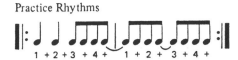

LATIN LOGIC

Moderate Latin Rock (play ♪♪ evenly)

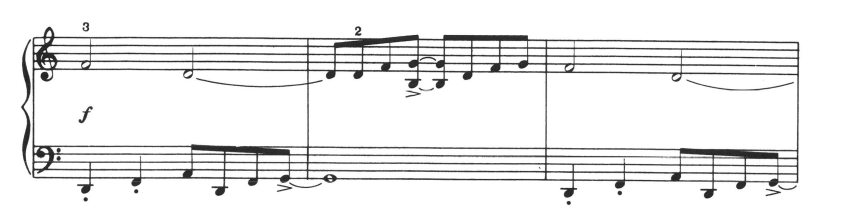

WALTZ FOR AMY

Practice rhythms

HANG OUT

Fast Rock Tempo (play ♪♪ evenly)

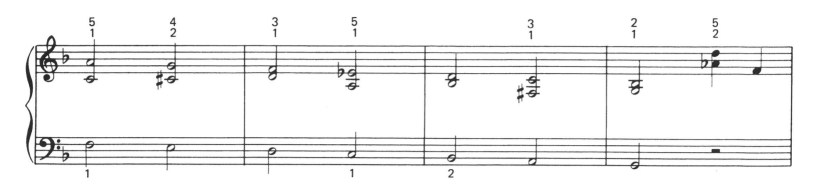

Practice Rhythms

IN A LATIN ROCK MOOD

NOTHIN' COULD BE FINER THAN MINOR

The grace notes are to be played on the beat, together with the principal note and then stopped immediately allowing the principal note to sound alone.

COMPOSER SHOWCASE
HAL LEONARD STUDENT PIANO LIBRARY

This series showcases great original piano music from our **Hal Leonard Student Piano Library** family of composers. Carefully graded for easy selection.

BILL BOYD

JAZZ BITS (AND PIECES)
Early Intermediate Level
00290312 11 Solos.....................$7.99

JAZZ DELIGHTS
Intermediate Level
00240435 11 Solos.....................$8.99

JAZZ FEST
Intermediate Level
00240436 10 Solos.....................$8.99

JAZZ PRELIMS
Early Elementary Level
00290032 12 Solos.....................$7.99

JAZZ SKETCHES
Intermediate Level
00220001 8 Solos.......................$8.99

JAZZ STARTERS
Elementary Level
00290425 10 Solos.....................$8.99

JAZZ STARTERS II
Late Elementary Level
00290434 11 Solos.....................$7.99

JAZZ STARTERS III
Late Elementary Level
00290465 12 Solos.....................$8.99

THINK JAZZ!
Early Intermediate Level
00290417 Method Book...........$12.99

TONY CARAMIA

JAZZ MOODS
Intermediate Level
00296728 8 Solos.......................$6.95

SUITE DREAMS
Intermediate Level
00296775 4 Solos.......................$6.99

SONDRA CLARK

DAKOTA DAYS
Intermediate Level
00296521 5 Solos.......................$6.95

FLORIDA FANTASY SUITE
Intermediate Level
00296766 3 Duets.....................$7.95

THREE ODD METERS
Intermediate Level
00296472 3 Duets.....................$6.95

MATTHEW EDWARDS

**CONCERTO FOR
YOUNG PIANISTS**
FOR 2 PIANOS, FOUR HANDS
Intermediate Level Book/CD
00296356 3 Movements $19.99

CONCERTO NO. 2 IN G MAJOR
FOR 2 PIANOS, 4 HANDS
Intermediate Level Book/CD
00296670 3 Movements...........$17.99

PHILLIP KEVEREN

MOUSE ON A MIRROR
Late Elementary Level
00296361 5 Solos.......................$8.99

MUSICAL MOODS
Elementary/Late Elementary Level
00296714 7 Solos.......................$6.99

SHIFTY-EYED BLUES
Late Elementary Level
00296374 5 Solos.......................$7.99

CAROL KLOSE

THE BEST OF CAROL KLOSE
Early to Late Intermediate Level
00146151 15 Solos....................$12.99

CORAL REEF SUITE
Late Elementary Level
00296354 7 Solos.......................$7.50

DESERT SUITE
Intermediate Level
00296667 6 Solos.......................$7.99

FANCIFUL WALTZES
Early Intermediate Level
00296473 5 Solos.......................$7.95

GARDEN TREASURES
Late Intermediate Level
00296787 5 Solos.......................$8.50

ROMANTIC EXPRESSIONS
Intermediate to Late Intermediate Level
00296923 5 Solos.......................$8.99

WATERCOLOR MINIATURES
Early Intermediate Level
00296848 7 Solos.......................$7.99

JENNIFER LINN

AMERICAN IMPRESSIONS
Intermediate Level
00296471 6 Solos.......................$8.99

ANIMALS HAVE FEELINGS TOO
Early Elementary/Elementary Level
00147789 8 Solos.......................$8.99

AU CHOCOLAT
Late Elementary/Early Intermediate Level
00298110 7 Solos.......................$8.99

CHRISTMAS IMPRESSIONS
Intermediate Level
00296706 8 Solos.......................$8.99

JUST PINK
Elementary Level
00296722 9 Solos.......................$8.99

LES PETITES IMAGES
Late Elementary Level
00296664 7 Solos.......................$8.99

LES PETITES IMPRESSIONS
Intermediate Level
00296355 6 Solos.......................$8.99

REFLECTIONS
Late Intermediate Level
00296843 5 Solos.......................$8.99

TALES OF MYSTERY
Intermediate Level
00296769 6 Solos.......................$8.99

LYNDA LYBECK-ROBINSON

ALASKA SKETCHES
Early Intermediate Level
00119637 8 Solos.......................$8.99

AN AWESOME ADVENTURE
Late Elementary Level
00137563 8 Solos.......................$7.99

FOR THE BIRDS
Early Intermediate/Intermediate Level
00237078 9 Solos.......................$8.99

WHISPERING WOODS
Late Elementary Level
00275905 9 Solos.......................$8.99

MONA REJINO

CIRCUS SUITE
Late Elementary Level
00296665 5 Solos.......................$8.99

COLOR WHEEL
Early Intermediate Level
00201951 6 Solos.......................$9.99

IMPRESIONES DE ESPAÑA
Intermediate Level
00337520 6 Solos.......................$8.99

IMPRESSIONS OF NEW YORK
Intermediate Level
00364212....................................$8.99

JUST FOR KIDS
Elementary Level
00296840 8 Solos.......................$7.99

MERRY CHRISTMAS MEDLEYS
Intermediate Level
00296799 5 Solos.......................$8.99

MINIATURES IN STYLE
Intermediate Level
00148088 6 Solos.......................$8.99

PORTRAITS IN STYLE
Early Intermediate Level
00296507 6 Solos.......................$8.99

EUGÉNIE ROCHEROLLE

CELEBRATION SUITE
Intermediate Level
00152724 3 Duets.....................$8.99

**ENCANTOS ESPAÑOLES
(SPANISH DELIGHTS)**
Intermediate Level
00125451 6 Solos.......................$8.99

JAMBALAYA
Intermediate Level
00296654 2 Pianos, 8 Hands.....$12.99
00296725 2 Pianos, 4 Hands.......$7.95

JEROME KERN CLASSICS
Intermediate Level
00296577 10 Solos....................$12.99

LITTLE BLUES CONCERTO
Early Intermediate Level
00142801 2 Pianos, 4 Hands......$12.99

TOUR FOR TWO
Late Elementary Level
00296832 6 Duets.....................$9.99

TREASURES
Late Elementary/Early Intermediate Level
00296924 7 Solos.......................$8.99

JEREMY SISKIND

BIG APPLE JAZZ
Intermediate Level
00278209 8 Solos.......................$8.99

MYTHS AND MONSTERS
Late Elementary/Early Intermediate Level
00148148 9 Solos.......................$8.99

CHRISTOS TSITSAROS

**DANCES FROM AROUND
THE WORLD**
Early Intermediate Level
00296688 7 Solos.......................$8.99

FIVE SUMMER PIECES
Late Intermediate/Advanced Level
00361235 5 Solos.......................$12.99

LYRIC BALLADS
Intermediate/Late Intermediate Level
00102404 6 Solos.......................$8.99

POETIC MOMENTS
Intermediate Level
00296403 8 Solos.......................$8.99

SEA DIARY
Early Intermediate Level
00253486 9 Solos.......................$8.99

SONATINA HUMORESQUE
Late Intermediate Level
00296772 3 Movements.............$6.99

SONGS WITHOUT WORDS
Intermediate Level
00296506 9 Solos.......................$9.99

THREE PRELUDES
Early Advanced Level
00130747 3 Solos.......................$8.99

THROUGHOUT THE YEAR
Late Elementary Level
00296723 12 Duets....................$6.95

ADDITIONAL COLLECTIONS

AT THE LAKE
by Elvina Pearce
Elementary/Late Elementary Level
00131642 10 Solos and Duets.....$7.99

CHRISTMAS FOR TWO
by Dan Fox
Early Intermediate Level
00290069 13 Duets....................$8.99

CHRISTMAS JAZZ
by Mike Springer
Intermediate Level
00296525 6 Solos.......................$8.99

COUNTY RAGTIME FESTIVAL
by Fred Kern
Intermediate Level
00296882 7 Solos.......................$7.99

LITTLE JAZZERS
by Jennifer Watts
Elementary/Late Elementary Level
00154573 9 Solos.......................$8.99

PLAY THE BLUES!
by Luann Carman
Early Intermediate Level
00296357 10 Solos....................$9.99

ROLLER COASTERS & RIDES
by Jennifer & Mike Watts
Intermediate Level
00131144 8 Duets.....................$8.99

www.halleonard.com

Prices, contents, and availability subject to change without notice.